Relevant Leadership Revolutionary Results Workbook

Leading in Life, Home, and Work

Dr. Bobbie Sparks

Relevant Leadership Revolutionary Results Workbook

Copyright © 2015 Time and Eternity

Published by Time and Eternity, www.timeandeternity.net, info@timeandeternity.net.

All Scripture quotations are taken from either the English Standard Version, © 2002 by Crossway Bibles or the King James Version, © 1987 by Biblegateway.com. Used by permission. All rights reserved.

Time and Eternity does not represent Wornick Foods.
It is a separate entity, non-related.

Time & Eternity Leadership Series

www.TELeadership.com

TABLE OF CONTENTS

Relevant Leadership Revolutionary Results Workbook

How To Use This Book

This workbook is meant to inspire growth, pinpoint areas to be developed, and encourage you to think through questions that will spur you on to being a better leader. This workbook is not all-encompassing, and in fact, you'll find a series of blanks at the end of each section for you to write your own questions and explore the depths of your thoughts as you use these principals in your surroundings.

Whether you're a CEO of a major corporation, a cook at a fast-food restaurant, a stay-at-home mom, a retiree, or anything and everything in between, there are truths that you can glean from this information and our hope is that these questions will cause you to really think. Take your time in answering these questions. It will do you no good to simply answer yes or no. If you really want to grow and change, invest time in yourself as you contemplate your answers and how you can really improve yourself and those around you. Your engagement with this material will determine the outcome of what you get. Be real, be vulnerable, and be willing to develop in every area of your life. Let's get started.

Chapter 1
Introduction

As we enter into this workbook, we'd like to take you through some questions to help you set expectations and be able to see where you are currently before we proceed.

1.) Who are some people that you are following currently?

_____

_____

_____

_____

_____

_____

2.) Who are some people in your past or historical figures that you admire for their leadership roles?

_____

_____

_____

_____

_____

_____

3.) What is your current definition of a leader and what are some characteristics of a good leader?

_____

_____

_____

_____

_____

_____

4.) What would you consider to be characteristics of a bad leader?

_____

_____

_____

_____

_____

_____

5.) Who are some people that are currently following you?

_____

_____

_____

_____

_____

_____

6.) How would you explain the difference between managing and leading?

_____

_____

_____

7.) What roles in your life require you to take leadership within the areas of life, home, and work? How do you feel you do in each of those roles?

_____

_____

_____

_____

_____

_____

8.) In walking through the 12 takeaways, in which pieces do you feel you will need to grow more and in which ones do you feel more confident? Why?

_____

_____

_____

_____

_____

_____

_____

_____

_____

_____

9.) Please rank the following from easiest for you to do to hardest: planning, following through, and adjusting to needed changes.

    1.

    2.

    3.

10.) For the hardest selection, what methods have you tried to improve in this area before that have and have not worked for you?

_____

_____

_____

_____

_____

_____

_____

_____

_____

11.) What are you hoping to gain from this book?

_____

_____

_____

_____

_____

_____

_____

_____

Here's where you can write your own questions.

Personal Reflection Questions:

12.) _____

_____

_____

_____

_____

_____

_____

_____

_____

_____

_____

_____

_____

13.) _____

_____

_____

_____

_____

_____

_____

_____

_____

_____

_____

_____

_____

_____

_____

Chapter 2
Nehemiah 1
Getting Started

In getting into this chapter, it's recommended that you take some time to read through the book of Nehemiah in the Bible. If you don't have one, it's easy to find a copy online at BibleGateway.com or through a general search. If you read 2 chapters a day, you'll be finished in less than 1 week and you'll have a better understanding of the story that we are drawing from.

1.) What areas of life, home, or work do you currently have a "why" for? Share those.

_____

_____

_____

_____

_____

_____

_____

_____

2.) What areas do you need to develop or think through a "why" for?

_____

_____

_____

_____

_____

_____

_____

_____

_____

3.) What is your:

    a.) Life Purpose Statement:

_____

_____

_____

_____

_____

_____

    b.) Home Purpose Statement

_____

_____

_____

_____

_____

_____

    c.) Work Purpose Statement:

_____

_____

_____

_____

_____

4.) Who or what is your anchor when the storms of life rage upon you?

_____

_____

_____

_____

_____

_____

_____

_____

5.) Do you know any examples of leaders being pathfinders? How did their leadership differ from that of a dictator boss?

_____

_____

_____

_____

_____

_____

_____

_____

6.) Do you have 1, 3, and 5-year goals that are in line with your hoshin or True North?
   a.   1 year:

_____

_____

_____

_____

   b.   3 year:

_____

_____

_____

_____

c. 5 year:

_____

_____

_____

_____

7.) Are those who are affected by your goals, or a part of them, aware of these goals and on board with them? Have you effectively communicated what they are?

_____

_____

_____

_____

_____

8.) Leadership involves seeing a need or purpose within your business, organization, church, or life and taking steps to move forward to fulfill it. What are some unmet needs that you currently see that you can be a part of meeting?

_____

_____

_____

_____

_____

_____

_____

_____

_____

9.) Among those working around you, with whom you do you need to intentionally build up and foster relationships? Example: I need to help develop my secretary so that she can speak with confidence, have the ability to work more efficiently using different tools, feel appreciated, and move up and train others in her field.

_____

_____

_____

_____

_____

_____

_____

10.) Within organizations, it is important for each individual's skill set to be well matched to his responsibilities, although this is often not found to be the case. For example, Bob joined a company to work as a computer programmer. After a few years, the company faced some tough times and Bob ended up working in the office helping with IT problems throughout the office. Jana was hired for IT, but because of her outspoken nature has been give more roles in programming, which she doesn't enjoy. It would be wise for a company to look at these two people and switch Bob back to Programming and allow Jana to focus on the IT solutions she enjoys. Identify areas in your organization where someone is doing a job that they are not naturally gifted in. Is there someone who could be filling that role more effectively?

_____

_____

_____

_____

_____

_____

_____

_____

11.) We mentioned being on time being a show of respect to others. What are other ways we can express respect on a daily basis?.

_____

_____

_____

_____

_____

_____

_____

12.) On a scale from 1-10, how would you rate your ability to manage time well so that you get tasks complete and are able to spend time on things that are important to you? Why did you write that number?

_____

_____

_____

_____

_____

_____

_____

13.) What are some ways you can adjust your time, if needed, to put your priorities first? Even during busy seasons, if you communicate well, you can find out what is most important and make it a priority.

_____

_____

_____

_____

_____

_____

_____

14.) The water cooler has gotten a bad reputation over the years as being the place where people congregate and gossip. Even if your organization has no water cooler, you may have negative environments. What are things you can do to change these environments in order to invite conversations that are more positive and genuine?

_____

_____

_____

_____

_____

_____

_____

15.) Tell an example of a situation that seemed really big that turned out to have a simple solution. How did you feel when the problem arose, while you were dealing with the problem, and after the solution?

_____

_____

_____

_____

_____

_____

_____

16.) What, if anything, is holding you back from being the leader that you could be or want to be?

_____

_____

_____

_____

_____

_____

Personal Reflection Questions:

17.) _____

_____

_____

_____

_____

_____

_____

_____

_____

_____

18.) _____

_____

_____

_____

_____

_____

_____

_____

_____

_____

Chapter 3
Nehemiah 2:1-10
Business Plan

In order to take a plan and make it happen, the foundation must be laid. This foundation will look different depending on circumstances and the plan being enacted, but the groundwork must be thoroughly complete. Avoid the temptation to jump to further steps without taking care of details that will cost you time and resources later.

1.) What are the costs that will be involved in the plan you are trying to accomplish?

_____

_____

_____

_____

_____

_____

_____

2.) What pressures and difficulties do you expect you may face as you move forward in your plan? How will you respond to them?

_____

_____

_____

_____

_____

_____

_____

_____

_____

_____

3.) Who do you need to approach about your goal for favor/approval/or confirmation? If you have done this before, how did the conversation go?

_____

_____

_____

_____

_____

4.) What are some things that you constantly talk about in a positive way? If you're not sure, ask someone. Are you effectively communicating a passion about the things that are important to you?

_____

_____

_____

_____

_____

_____

_____

5.) When expressing the passion you have about something to get others involved, be sure to express the "why" so that they see your heart. How would you invite someone to be a part of your passion?

_____

_____

_____

_____

_____

_____

_____

_____

6.) In presenting ideas, do you tend to share with everyone or those that need to hear? Be wary of over-sharing which can in return give you negative feedback and cause doubts. Has this ever happened to you or someone you know? Tell us about it.

_____

_____

_____

_____

_____

_____

7.) As you plan and execute plans, how clearly can you explain what you want, how long it will take, and what you will need to see it through to completion? Which part of your plan do you need help with, if any? Share.

_____

_____

_____

_____

_____

_____

_____

_____

8.) Do you have any dreams or plans that require you to take action or walk away? Sometimes we hang on to dreams or plans just because they're familiar to us. Sometimes we hang on to them in fear of stepping out and making them happen. Sometimes we need to just wait. Where do you fit in this?

_____

_____

_____

_____

_____

_____

_____

_____

_____

9.) Have you missed any opportunities because you were not prepared to step through the door that was opened to you? What caused you to miss them?

_____

_____

_____

_____

_____

_____

_____

_____

10.) What things do you need to address that have held you back in the past so that they don't continue to have a hold on you now or in the future?

_____

_____

_____

_____

_____

_____

_____

_____

_____

11.) Are there opportunities that you were ready for and stepped into eagerly? How did you prepare and respond to these?

_____

_____

_____

_____

_____

_____

12.) How willing are you to step up and take the lead when you see a need? What reservations or enthusiasm do you have in response to this question?

_____

_____

_____

_____

_____

_____

13.) Being aware of the tendencies of your team members working style will help you to understand and cooperate with each other better. What kind of working style do you have? When you start a project, do you tend to prepare in advance or go with the flow? Do you tend to complete projects or leave things unfinished?

_____

_____

_____

_____

_____

_____

14.) When managing short-term and long-term projects, do you find it easiest to start, work on, or finish a task?

_____

_____

_____

_____

_____

_____

_____

15.) As you implement plans, do you communicate your expectations well? How can you improve in communication or help others improve? What are some effective ways you have seen expectations being communicated?

_____

_____

_____

_____

_____

_____

16.) How do you respond to opposition of your plans? When things don't go as you desire, what are some good strategies to help you and others respond to the change?

_____

_____

_____

_____

_____

_____

_____

Personal Reflection Questions:

17.) _____

_____

_____

_____

_____

_____

_____

_____

_____

_____

_____

_____

_____

_____

18.) _____

_____

_____

_____

_____

_____

_____

_____

Chapter 4
Nehemiah 2:11-20
Beginning Steps

Now that you have a good idea of what your plan is, have a solid foundation, and are prepared for opposition, it's time to start moving forward. Gathering information to support your vision is a great place to start. The more information you can gather, the better off you'll be.

1.) What information do you need to gather in order to present and accomplish your plan or goal?

_____

_____

_____

_____

_____

2.) Before you even begin your project, you may be aware of some problems that you will encounter along the way. What information will you need to gather in order to address those problems? For example, as you start a snow cone business, a potential problem you might face is an ice machine breakdown. Some information you could gather to address that problem would be finding a trustworthy repairman and making initial contact with him.

_____

_____

_____

_____

_____

3.) What does going to the gemba look like in your life?

_____

_____

_____

_____

_____

_____

_____

4.) When you are approached about a problem, how do you typically respond? Do you go to the problem to see it? Can you share an example where a problem was made worse by someone not going to address the problem?

_____

_____

_____

_____

_____

5.) How often do you take time away from "doing" to reflect on what has been done, what is going on, and what problems have crept in? How would taking time to reflect be helpful to you?

_____

_____

_____

_____

_____

6.) How can you schedule in time for reflection? What are you going to do during this time?

_____

_____

_____

_____

_____

7.) When problems come up, what are ways you can:
  a. Include yourself in the solution:

  _____

  _____

  _____

  _____

  _____

  _____

  b. Speak of a greater purpose:

  _____

  _____

  _____

  _____

  _____

  _____

  c. Remind people or yourself of past times where things worked out:

  _____

  _____

  _____

  _____

  d. End with an appeal for unity:

  _____

  _____

  _____

  _____

  _____

8.) How can it be helpful to be reminded of the goal that you're working towards? What happens when you lose sight of the "why?"

_____

_____

_____

_____

_____

_____

_____

9.) How important is it that a vision is cast for others to be a part of whether at home, life, or work? How can speaking your goals help invite others in?

_____

_____

_____

_____

10.) What are some things that you can do to communicate your vision or goals in order to allow others to join you in support?

_____

_____

_____

_____

_____

_____

_____

11.) Doubt has a way of finding its way into our lives. How have you seen doubt and fear create problems in your own life or in the lives of others?

_____

_____

_____

_____

_____

12.) What do you usually do when you are slipping into times of doubt? What standard could you set for how you want to respond during these times?

_____

_____

_____

_____

_____

_____

13.) What is your plan for when you face fear? Share that with others.

_____

_____

_____

_____

_____

_____

_____

_____

14.) Doug was encouraged by Rudyard Kipling's poem *If* (pg. 83). In reading through this poem, what pieces inspire you, challenge you, or speak to you?

_____

_____

_____

_____

_____

_____

_____

_____

_____

Personal Reflection Questions:

15.) _____

_____

_____

_____

_____

_____

_____

_____

_____

_____

_____

_____

_____

16.) _____

_____

_____

_____

_____

_____

_____

_____

_____

_____

_____

_____

_____

_____

_____

_____

Chapter 5
Nehemiah 3
The Setup

The outline has been set, foundation secure, and you're ready to get into pieces that you're excited about. The "doing" part of a plan is often the easiest for many, at least getting started in the doing. From this chapter on, we'll be referring to PDCA often. This cycle is like the wheel that keeps you moving forward. There is no reverse to the PDCA process. If done well, or at least decently, it will help you generate forward momentum that will cause change. After some practice, it will become subconscious as you check yourself and others against a plan to see if progress is being made, and if not, you'll find out why and adjust the plan.

1.) What does the acronym PDCA stand for? Pg. 89

P _____

D _____

C _____

A _____

2.) As you think about your plan or goal, what is your starting point? Does it align with your hoshin (True North)?

_____

_____

_____

_____

_____

_____

_____

_____

_____

_____

3.) Share what you believe your roles are. What do you expect from yourself within those roles?

_____

_____

_____

_____

_____

4.) Can you share a story of someone being hurt or angry because another person did not meet an expectation they had because the person didn't understand that it was their role to do it?

_____

_____

_____

_____

_____

_____

_____

_____

_____

_____

_____

_____

5.) How would clearly defined roles save time and effort?

_____

_____

_____

_____

_____

_____

6.)   Give an example of when you focused on yourself and therefore caused others to do more work or struggle.

_____

_____

_____

_____

_____

_____

_____

7.)   Are you a team player or do you tend to become self-focused? What are ways you can help build up the team that you have?

_____

_____

_____

_____

_____

8.)   How would others define your role? Do you know what others expect from you?

_____

_____

_____

_____

_____

_____

9.) Why is it that the more responsibility one has, the smaller the percentage of their role is defined? See page 94 if you need to refresh your memory.

_____

_____

_____

_____

_____

_____

_____

10.) How could the PDCA process help both the motivated and less motivated stay on target?

_____

_____

_____

_____

_____

11.) As a leader, how often are you working alongside those you are in charge of instead of being a taskmaster? Do your people know that you are working with them and not over them? How can you make sure they do?

_____

_____

_____

_____

_____

_____

_____

12.) What does this statement mean to you: "When you understand who you are, what you are and where you are no longer makes as much difference?"

_____

_____

_____

_____

_____

_____

13.) How are you doing in including those important to you in your plan and time? How would they say you are doing?

_____

_____

_____

_____

_____

_____

14.) What does the completion of your plan look like? How will you know when you have completed it?

_____

_____

_____

_____

_____

_____

15.) What fundamentals do you need to remember and begin practicing again?

_____

_____

_____

_____

_____

16.) What changes are you excited about making?

_____

_____

_____

_____

_____

_____

_____

_____

_____

Personal Reflection Questions:

17.) _____

_____

_____

_____

_____

_____

_____

_____

_____

_____

_____

_____

_____

18.) _____

_____

_____

_____

_____

_____

_____

_____

_____

_____

_____

_____

_____

Chapter 6
Nehemiah 4:1-15
When Things Get Tough

Being faced with opposition forces us to respond or react. There are good ways to respond and there are poor ways to react along with a whole list in between. Having a plan in place to help you face difficulties will help you make better decisions when emotions are at a high and mistakes could easily be made.

1.) How have you dealt with opposition or conflict in the past? Can you share a story of a time when you responded well or reacted poorly?

_____

_____

_____

_____

_____

_____

2.) When opposition plays on your insecurities and fears, what are some things you can do to clear your mind so that you can make a good decision on responding?

_____

_____

_____

_____

_____

_____

_____

_____

_____

3.) Sometimes opposition comes from people close to you. Sometimes winning an argument means losing a friend. How can you respond in such a way that you come to a common understanding and maintain the relationship? Is it always possible to do so?

_____

_____

_____

_____

_____

_____

_____

4.) Nehemiah was faced with many false accusations. Instead of fighting back in order to try to gain justice on his own, how did he respond? What does it look like for you to respond similarly in your life?

_____

_____

_____

_____

_____

_____

_____

5.) Often our society tells us that if we don't fight back, we will get run over. How does Nehemiah's response to not fight for his rights speak to this belief?

_____

_____

_____

_____

_____

6.) Tell about a time when you or someone you know was falsely accused? What was the reaction from all who were involved?

_____

_____

_____

_____

_____

_____

_____

7.) What are some good ways that you can respond to false accusations without becoming defensive?

_____

_____

_____

_____

_____

_____

_____

8.) Describe a situation you have been in where people around you only dragged you down. What feelings did this invoke in you?

_____

_____

_____

_____

_____

_____

_____

9.) Having a reason to show up every day provides some accountability in what you're doing. What are some ways or people that keep you accountable to show up and be present?

_____

_____

_____

_____

_____

_____

_____

10.) Why is it important for a leader to be consistent in being there and being on time? How does it affect others?

_____

_____

_____

_____

_____

_____

_____

11.) Who do you have in your life as an encouragement?   What is it about this person or people that refreshes you? Do you make it a priority to spend time with them?

_____

_____

_____

_____

_____

_____

_____

12.) Maybe you do pretty well in not being discouraged often and not feeling the need to fight back out of defensiveness. If this is the case, how are you doing in coaching others to do the same?

_____

_____

_____

_____

_____

_____

13.) What are the 5S's? Check page 107 if you need to.

_____

_____

_____

_____

_____

14.) How can a system like 5S diminish some of the smaller frustrations of daily life? How could you implement 5S in your situation? How often do you have to search for things that are missing such as keys, scissors, tools, etc...?

_____

_____

_____

_____

_____

_____

15.) What fears or doubts do you need to address in your own life?

_____

_____

_____

_____

_____

_____

_____

16.) Do you need to talk to someone about addressing their fears and doubts? With whom and when will you do that?

_____

_____

_____

_____

_____

_____

_____

17.) Think of some groups of people that you interact with on a regular basis. What are ways that you could help unify the people within these groups?

_____

_____

_____

_____

_____

_____

18.) Leading in some situations can feel very awkward and isolating. Addressing rumors or gossip can be one of those times. What are ways that you can you speak up in these situations in order to end the false talk while strengthening your relationships with those involved?

_____

_____

_____

_____

_____

_____

19.) In your own journey of growth, what have been some catalysts for positive change that led to peaks in your growth?

_____

_____

_____

_____

_____

_____

_____

_____

_____

_____

_____

_____

_____

20.) Do you see any common patterns that led to moments of decline or stagnant growth that you could avoid in the future?

_____

_____

_____

_____

_____

_____

_____

_____

Personal Reflection Questions:

21.) _____

_____

_____

_____

_____

_____

_____

_____

_____

_____

_____

_____

_____

22.) _____

_____

_____

_____

_____

_____

_____

_____

_____

_____

_____

_____

_____

_____

_____

_____

Chapter 7
Nehemiah 4:16-23
PDCA and Problem Solving

1.) Have you begun using PDCA in your life? If so, share some of your experiences.

_____

_____

_____

_____

_____

_____

_____

_____

_____

_____

_____

2.) Which pieces of the PDCA process are harder for you?

_____

_____

_____

_____

3.) How often do you check your plan to see what needs to be adjusted?

_____

_____

_____

_____

4.) Page 115-116 talks about Personal Protection Equipment tools to help you protect yourself or others. What are ways that you physically protect yourself? What are ways that you mentally protect yourself?

_____

_____

_____

_____

_____

_____

5.) What are some things that tend to hinder your progress? What have you done in the past to help you overcome these or other hindrances?

_____

_____

_____

_____

6.) Ralph Waldo Emerson said, 'Your actions speak so loudly, I cannot hear what you are saying." What would those closest to you say that your life speaks of?

_____

_____

_____

_____

_____

_____

7.)   What are some areas in which you are tempted to slack off that could later cause problems or cause others to slack off because of your example?

_____

_____

_____

_____

_____

8.)   Are there some audible or visual controls that you can set into place to remind you of things that need to be happening?

_____

_____

_____

_____

_____

_____

9.)   What are some audible and visual controls that you respond to on a daily basis? How do these help you function in life and society?

_____

_____

_____

_____

_____

_____

_____

10.) Do you have some type of audible or visual control to call attention to your needs personally or professionally? If yes, what are they and how do you use them? If not, what could they be and how would they be helpful?

_____

_____

_____

_____

_____

_____

_____

11.) If you choose not to respond to the controls around you, how does that affect others around you?

_____

_____

_____

_____

_____

_____

_____

12.) Andon signals alert you of a need for help. We have andon signals internally and externally. When you feel your heart begin to race, your andon signal is telling you to take a step back from the situation and regain composure. This is an example of an internal andon signal. What are some of your personal internal andon signals?

_____

_____

_____

_____

_____

_____

_____

13.) Do you feel comfortable asking for help when mistakes are made? If yes, what helps you remain comfortable? If no, what about the situation makes you uncomfortable?

_____

_____

_____

_____

_____

_____

_____

14.) How can you be a safe person for people to approach when they have made a mistake? What are some qualities of an approachable coach? What are some qualities of an angry dictator?

_____

_____

_____

_____

_____

_____

_____

15.) When you have personal andon signals going off left and right, how do you communicate that to those who are most important to you? Do you go to them for support, run from them, or respond another way? Why?

_____

_____

_____

_____

_____

_____

16.) What are some problem solving methods that you use or have seen used?

_____

_____

_____

_____

_____

_____

_____

17.) Do you have a problem solving method that you use to find the root of the problem rather than just the result? Which one are you using? If you don't have one, consider the 8 step problem solving method on page 119.

_____

_____

_____

_____

_____

_____

_____

18.) Can you share a time when the result of the problem was addressed instead of the root? How did it effect the relationships involved?

_____

_____

_____

_____

_____

_____

_____

19.) What are some benefits of addressing problems when they arise instead of avoiding the conflict?

_____

_____

_____

_____

_____

_____

_____

_____

Personal Reflection Questions:

20.) _____

_____

_____

_____

_____

_____

_____

_____

_____

_____

_____

_____

21.) _____

Chapter 8: Nehemiah 5
The Right Culture:
Building a Culture of Respect

Creating an environment, a common value system, and defining acceptable behaviors can be a difficult task. It is one, however, that is worth the time. Once a culture is created, it is sustainable through consistent development of people within that system. Building a culture of mutual respect allows for easier growth and development of all people.

1.) What adjectives would you use to describe the current culture of your home and work spaces?

_____

_____

_____

_____

_____

_____

2.) When you imagine your current culture as growing and flourishing, what adjectives would you use to describe it?

_____

_____

_____

_____

_____

_____

_____

_____

_____

_____

3.) What examples have you seen of how a negative culture impacts the quality of life of the people in it?

_____

_____

_____

_____

_____

_____

_____

_____

4.) Have you seen leadership address negative culture? What were their approaches and outcomes of the situation?

_____

_____

_____

_____

_____

_____

_____

_____

_____

_____

_____

_____

5.) Would you choose to take a lower paying position if it meant being in a culture where you were respected, valued, and encouraged on a regular basis? Why or why not?

_____

_____

_____

_____

_____

_____

_____

_____

6.) Are you oppressing people under you in fear that they will rise up and take your place or for another reason? Can you share an example of seeing this happen within yourself and others?

_____

_____

_____

_____

_____

_____

7.) Would you say that those you lead are put first? Would they say that?

_____

_____

_____

_____

_____

_____

8.) When you offer opportunities for those you lead to develop and grow, how does that affect the overall culture and motivation of the people? Why?

_____

_____

_____

_____

_____

_____

_____

_____

9.) Can you share an example of a leader providing you with an opportunity to develop and grow that made a big difference in your life?

_____

_____

_____

_____

_____

_____

_____

_____

10.) How would it change the situation if you were to focus your energy on solving the problem instead of attacking or blaming the person or people involved?

_____

_____

_____

_____

_____

_____
_____
_____
_____
_____

11.) Do you find it difficult to approach people when you need to have a difficult conversation ? If so, what brings out that fear? If not, what are some methods you use to do so?

_____
_____
_____
_____
_____
_____

12.) When you have standards in place that have been clearly communicated, how would that make difficult conversations easier to have and less personal?

_____
_____
_____
_____
_____
_____
_____
_____
_____

13.) Can you share an example of a person being promoted and getting a big head? How did that affect the relationships and respect of that person?

_____

_____

_____

_____

_____

_____

_____

14.) Can you share an example of a person being promoted and responding in humility and ownership of responsibility, confidence and servant leadership? How did that affect the relationships and respect of that person?

_____

_____

_____

_____

_____

_____

15.) How have you seen power of position being used incorrectly?

_____

_____

_____

_____

_____

_____

16.) When power of position is used to serve others, what difference does it make in those they serve?

_____

_____

_____

_____

_____

_____

_____

17.) How can privileges cause schisms in different situations?

_____

_____

_____

_____

_____

_____

_____

18.) Spend some time reflecting on your positions in life. Are you using those for the benefit of others so that you mutually prosper? Are you oppressing anyone in your life? Are you developing people without fear of being overthrown? Is there anything else you need to discuss or someone you need to make things right with?

_____

_____

_____

_____

_____

_____

_____

_____

_____

_____

_____

_____

_____

Personal Reflection Questions:

19.) _____

_____

_____

_____

_____

_____

_____

_____

_____

_____

_____

_____

_____

_____

20.) _____

_____

_____

_____

_____

_____

_____

_____

_____

_____

_____

_____

_____

_____

Chapter 9
Nehemiah 4:6
Don't Let Progress Be Your Downfall

So many people start something new with great vigor. There is excitement and energy generated to move forward to see the project through. Progress happens and for many, it comes with opposition that they were not prepared for. Before long, progress, which should be something we celebrate, comes with more pressure, increased busyness and a loss of perspective.

1.)   What reminders have you set up to ensure that you and those around you do not lose perspective and forget the "why?"

_____

_____

_____

_____

_____

_____

_____

2.)   Think of previous times when you or someone you know lost perspective in the midst of growth or busyness. What similarities can you draw from them that you could use as an indicator for future reference to keep the same from happening again?

_____

_____

_____

_____

_____

_____

_____

_____

3.) Who or what are external oppositions in your life? How can you respond so that it doesn't weigh you down?

_____

_____

_____

_____

_____

4.) When you are faced with accusations, false or otherwise, what is your initial reaction? Often that reaction is defensive. What would a response given with humility, transparency and honesty look like in different areas in your life? How can you compose yourself in order to take down the defense walls and have a conversation instead of an argument?

_____

_____

_____

_____

_____

_____

_____

_____

_____

_____

_____

_____

_____

_____

_____

5.) Who do you feel like you could approach for help when things go wrong or you mess up? Who would you be reluctant to approach? How can you emulate the approachable ones? What strategies can you use to deal with the less approachable ones?

_____

_____

_____

_____

_____

_____

_____

_____

_____

_____

6.) There will be days when good people have a bad day. They will respond at times with words that are hurtful, even unintentionally. How will you respond to times like these so that you don't lose a relationship because of a bad choice that was made?

_____

_____

_____

_____

_____

_____

_____

_____

_____

7.) What are some things that happen or words that are said that tend to cause you to be discouraged? Being aware of these things can help you identify them and protect you from them.

_____

_____

_____

_____

_____

_____

_____

8.) Sometimes information is received wrong because of personal filters. The news that the copier is broken will be much more difficult to take after having a car wreck that morning, spilling coffee on yourself, and making a big mistake at work after the night you'd just had when your newborn decided that sleeping was not on his agenda. What are things you can do to be sure that information is coming through as it was intended? Are there reminders that you can put into place to allow yourself time to get refocused before continuing?

_____

_____

_____

_____

_____

_____

_____

_____

_____

9.) Similarly, are you taking the time to recognize when others around you are having a difficult time? This can affect how they are receiving the information you are trying to convey. Can you share an example where this happened, positively or negatively?

_____

_____

_____

_____

_____

_____

_____

_____

_____

_____

10.) Do you often check in with others to see how they are doing at the cost of getting work done or are you more task oriented with a tendency to overlook the person and see only the results, or lack thereof, in their work? Do you need to strengthen your focus more on tasks or relationships? How will you do this?

_____

_____

_____

_____

_____

_____

_____

_____

11.) What was the purpose of the Ebenezer from 1 Samuel 7:12 (Pg. 140)? What are some Ebenezer's that you have set up in your life to remind you of accomplishments or difficult tasks that you overcame in your past?

_____
_____
_____
_____
_____
_____
_____

12.) What have you done or are you doing to acknowledge achievements in your own life and in the lives of others around you?

_____
_____
_____
_____
_____
_____
_____
_____

13.) "Resistance makes you stronger." Do you agree or disagree with this statement, why or why not?

_____
_____
_____
_____
_____
_____

14.) Problem firefighting means that you only deal with the result of the problems instead of addressing the core issue. Can you give examples of firefighting versus problem-solving?

_____

_____

_____

_____

_____

_____

_____

_____

_____

15.) The reward for doing your job well often means more responsibility. How have you seen this as true in your own life or in lives of others around you? Is this a good thing or bad? What makes you say that?

_____

_____

_____

_____

_____

_____

_____

_____

_____

16.) When you recognize or reward people for correcting issues, are you doing so for problem-solving or firefighting? How can you recognize the difference so that you reward the correct behavior?

_____

_____

_____

_____

_____

_____

_____

_____

_____

_____

Personal Reflection Questions:

17.) _____

_____

_____

_____

_____

_____

_____

_____

_____

_____

_____

_____

18.) _____

Chapter 10
Nehemiah 7-8
Engaging People

Engaging people in the processes and vision that you have is very important. It allows you to build a team that supports you, encourages you and improves the system that you have. When people are engaged, progress happens at a faster rate and the plan becomes more enjoyable for everyone involved.

1.) Think about some activities, jobs, or groups that you are engaged in. What about these things grabs your attention and causes you to be involved?

_____

_____

_____

_____

_____

_____

_____

2.) Leadership should communicate the vision and the roles necessary to accomplish it so that others can take part in what the organization is wanting to do. When leaders aren't communicating well, what are some ways you can approach them to obtain clarification?

_____

_____

_____

_____

_____

_____

_____

_____

_____

3.) What are some areas of your life that you want others to be engaged in within your work, home, interest groups, church, etc...? How can you invite others to engage in these things?

_____

_____

_____

_____

_____

_____

_____

_____

4.) Communication is much more than emitting a message. The receiver plays a huge role in how a message is truly communicated. If your invitation for engagement has not been effective, what are some ways that you can adapt it to meet your audience?

_____

_____

_____

_____

_____

_____

_____

_____

_____

_____

_____

5.) As you look at building a culture of people that you can engage in a specific vision or task, are you inviting people in who have the same mindset? What does that culture look like? Example: A basketball coach recruiting team oriented, fundamentally solid players versus looking for individual standouts in order to promote the culture he wants to create.

_____

_____

_____

_____

_____

_____

_____

_____

6.) Peter Schutz, former president and CEO of Porsche said, "Hire character, train skill." Training skills is easier than training the character of a person to meet your desired culture, but you must have a system of training in place that continue to promote both. What are some ways that you are helping people, or yourself, train for both character and skill? What are the desired outcomes? What plan can you put in place that can be checked to ensure progress is being made and easy to see?

_____

_____

_____

_____

_____

_____

_____

_____

_____

_____

7.) In what ways do you feel secure in your role and how has that benefited you? Example: Because my son is secure in his role in our family, he feels the freedom to tell me when he has made a mistake so that we can talk about ways to fix it.

_____

_____

_____

_____

_____

_____

_____

8.) What are ways that you can help provide security for others around you in their relationship with you? Do you need to improve on communication, how you respond to situations, create standards that are understood by all, or in other ways?

_____

_____

_____

_____

_____

_____

9.) Planning wisely protects you so that when difficult times come, you are able to keep your commitment to people and maintain security. Remember that when people are insecure, it breeds fear which often leads to poor decisions and bad attitudes. Do you have personal or professional examples of this?

_____

_____

_____

_____

_____

_____

10.) In working systems, it's easy to overlook those who deserve to be recognized. There are often people working very hard who aren't noticed because of a quieter personality or a lack of opportunities to be seen. How are you recognizing these silent heroes in your life personally or professionally so that they are encouraged and feel valued?

_____

_____

_____

_____

_____

_____

_____

_____

_____

11.) Many groups promote people based upon favoritism or relationships. As you recognize or promote people, what are characteristics you look for as a standard to keep this from happening?

_____

_____

_____

_____

_____

_____

_____

_____

_____

_____

_____

12.) What are your standards for awards and recognition at home, work or other areas of your life? Standards decrease jealousy and favoritism by acknowledging those who have earned it.

_____

_____

_____

_____

_____

_____

_____

_____

_____

13.) How often do you remind yourself or those around you of the hoshin? Why is this necessary?

_____

_____

_____

_____

_____

_____

14.) Who in your life do you need to take the time to communicate appreciation for? What is your plan for doing that?

_____

_____

_____

_____

_____

_____

_____

_____

_____

15.) Henry Ford said, "Coming together is a beginning, staying together is progress, and working together is success." How are you doing in working together successfully with those in differing roles in your life? How can your improve?

_____

_____

_____

_____

_____

_____

_____

16.) Recognizing improvement, remembering the purpose, and redefining the goal set before people is important to make sure that you stay on course for the desired goal. Do you have times set aside to celebrate growth in relationships, remind people of the purpose, and recommit to the vision in order to keep moving forward? What have these times looked like in the past and what are some ideas for doing so in the future?

_____

_____

_____

_____

_____

_____

_____

17.) How are you cultivating relationships in the midst of accomplishing tasks? What are some things you have done or seen others do to build stronger bonds with people?

_____

_____

_____

_____

_____

_____

_____

_____

_____

18.) How are you communicating thankfulness to other people, or how are you going to?

_____

_____

_____

_____

_____

_____

_____

_____

_____

19.) Random acts of kindness can change the entire atmosphere of a place. What are some things you can do for others this week that will build your relationships and help create an atmosphere of thankfulness?

_____

_____

_____

_____

_____

_____

_____

_____

20.) By this point in the book, you should have some plans in action. Take some time to check them. What things do you need to adapt in order to move forward?

_____

_____

_____

_____

_____

_____

_____

_____

_____

_____

_____

Personal Reflection Questions:

21.) _____

_____

_____

_____

_____

_____

_____

_____

_____

_____

_____

_____

_____

_____

_____

22.) _____

_____

_____

_____

_____

_____

_____

_____

Chapter 11
Nehemiah 9
Bringing the Culture to the Newbies

As time goes on, new people will be brought in to the culture you've worked hard to create. New relationships will be formed and changes will begin to happen. If you want to maintain the culture that you've worked to gain, you'll have to teach this culture to the new people joining in. Protecting the culture requires intentionality and continuous teaching. Without that, slowly the culture will begin to fade away and develop into something new. Small changes over a long period of time equal large changes.

1.) What are some characteristics of the culture that you have created around you? What characteristics do you want to ensure are instilled in others so that you can maintain or continue building the culture that you desire?

_____

_____

_____

_____

_____

_____

_____

2.) What does it mean to protect the culture? Why would it be important to do so?

_____

_____

_____

_____

_____

_____

_____

_____

3.) Is the culture around you progressing or have you seen old habits creep in?

_____

_____

_____

_____

_____

_____

4.) If you're seeing old habits come in, what are some areas of disconnect that are allowing this to take place?

_____

_____

_____

_____

_____

_____

_____

_____

_____

5.) On a regular basis, in what ways have you contributed to problems? In what ways have you contributed to solutions? What makes you respond this way? Can you give some examples?

_____

_____

_____

_____

_____

_____

6.) Many times when things are going well, people tend to slack off and slowly progress stops being made. Can you share an example of this happening?

_____

_____

_____

_____

_____

_____

7.) As new people come into your organization, family, or group, what are you doing to teach them the history and help them understand the process of how you got where you currently are?

_____

_____

_____

_____

_____

_____

8.) Are you assessing expectations and making sure that everyone is going in the same direction?

_____

_____

_____

_____

_____

_____

_____

Personal Reflection Questions:

9.) _____

_____

_____

_____

_____

_____

_____

_____

_____

_____

_____

_____

_____

_____

10.) _____

_____

_____

_____

_____

_____

_____

_____

_____

_____

_____

_____

Chapter 12
Nehemiah 10
Commitment and Trust

Commitment is a word that many people shy away from. In today's world, it's difficult to find people willing to commit to anything long-term. The "Bureau of Labor Statistics in 2012 showed that people from the ages of 25 to 34 years old were staying at their current job for approximately 3.2 years" (Sloan 2014). With statistics like these, it makes it hard for both the employee and the employer to trust each other. The same commitment problem can be seen through other areas of life outside of work. In order to maintain growth, there must be a level of commitment and trust that is established. Communication of expectations and development plans are more important than ever. In this section, really take some time to look at your own commitment and trust levels in the relationships in your life.

1.) Would you consider yourself to be a committed person? What would others around you say, and why?

_____

_____

_____

_____

_____

_____

2.) Do you know the commitment level of the people around you? What factors do you use to determine their commitment?

_____

_____

_____

_____

_____

_____

3.) How are you doing in checking in with where people are in their commitment levels? How often will you do this?

_____

_____

_____

_____

_____

_____

_____

4.) When changes are made, are they communicated well and expectations adjusted based upon the change?

_____

_____

_____

_____

_____

_____

_____

_____

5.) How committed are you to making others successful? Why do you have this commitment and how do you show it?

_____

_____

_____

_____

_____

_____

_____

6.) As you think about your own development, what are some areas in which you want to gain skills or abilities? Do you have a plan to make that happen?

_____

_____

_____

_____

_____

_____

_____

7.) As you develop others, do you know the skills they need to gain to improve and have a plan for that to happen in a reasonable amount of time?

_____

_____

_____

_____

_____

_____

_____

8.) What are your personal progress goals? Who will you share these goals with for accountability and encouragement?

_____

_____

_____

_____

_____

_____

9.) When you leave a place or a group, either momentarily or over a longer period of time, such as for a vacation, do you feel confident that the culture and progress continues just as well without your presence? Explain.

_____

_____

_____

_____

_____

_____

10.) When people around you fail, how do you respond? Are they able to leave your presence built up or torn down?

_____

_____

_____

_____

_____

_____

_____

_____

11.) Small issues can become big problems if they are consistently not addressed. Are there any small issues in your life that you're overlooking hoping they will go away? What are they and what will you do about them?

_____

_____

_____

_____

_____

_____

12.) What are ways that you are giving back to others? How does this build trust?

_____

_____

_____

_____

_____

_____

13.) Do you know of any examples where giving was viewed poorly because some felt neglected or not taken care of first?

_____

_____

_____

_____

_____

_____

14.) What are some ways that you are currently giving back or can give back to those around you? As an individual? As a group?

_____

_____

_____

_____

_____

_____

Personal Reflection Questions:

15.) _____

_____

_____

_____

_____

_____

_____

_____

_____

_____

_____

_____

_____

_____

16.) _____

_____

_____

_____

_____

_____

_____

_____

_____

_____

_____

Chapter 13
Nehemiah 11
Building New Leadership

Training new leadership to take on responsibilities should be a constant, ongoing part of your life regardless of what roles you fill. You should always be on the lookout for those that you can help develop and bring out their fullest potential. If you only lead by creating followers and not leaders, then the whole operation will crumble when you're not there. Building leaders allow for processes, cultures, characteristics, and systems to continue beyond a single leader.

1.) Genuine leaders are constantly sacrificing for others. Think about some leaders who have impacted you. What sacrifices have they made so that you could benefit from them?

_____

_____

_____

_____

_____

_____

2.) "Decisions made out of genuine care for others establishes an environment that spurs growth for everyone involved." How would these decisions create an environment where people have an opportunity to grow?

_____

_____

_____

_____

_____

_____

_____

3.)   What is the point of developing people if they are simply going to leave and go to another place?

_____

_____

_____

_____

_____

_____

4.)   When you have clear, defined roles and responsibilities, how can that help decrease stress and pressure? Do you have any examples?

_____

_____

_____

_____

_____

_____

_____

_____

_____

_____

5.)   Explain how a defined role would allow for a progression path that you can PDCA to ensure that you're moving forward.

_____

_____

_____

_____

_____

_____

_____

6.) "Be sure that you are developing the person and not just the skills." What does this mean to you and how have you seen this done before?

_____

_____

_____

_____

_____

_____

_____

7.) Describe what an attitude of thankfulness looks like in your current life state?

_____

_____

_____

_____

_____

_____

8.) List 20 things that you are genuinely thankful for.

1. _____

2. _____

3. _____

4. _____

5. _____

6. _____

7. _____

8. _____

9. _____

10. _____

11. _____

12. _____

13. _____

14. _____

15. _____

16. _____

17. _____

18. _____

19. _____

20. _____

9.) Are there some people that you need to talk to after writing this list who would be encouraged by your words of gratitude towards them? Who are they and when are you going to do this?

_____

_____

_____

_____

_____

_____

_____

_____

10.) "Communicating effectively should produce positive emotional responses to new tasks or changes." When you have discussions with people, do they leave your presence more equipped and confident to handle the task before them or do they feel berated and inadequate? The words you use can make a big difference on the changes that result from your conversations. Can you share some personal experiences of this, both good and bad?

_____

_____

_____

_____

_____

_____

_____

_____

_____

11.) There are people who may bring you down very easily. For some, even their very presence stirs anger or discouragement in your heart. Sometimes these people can be avoided, but not always. Can you set up road blocks to protect yourself from being with this kind of person for extended periods of time? What would that look like for you? Do they have this affect on you because of your tendencies or because of a characteristic that they have?

_____

_____

_____

_____

_____

_____

12.) Do you sense when others are discouraged or brought down because of what people around them say or do? Are you protecting them from these influences that cause harm to them?

_____

_____

_____

_____

_____

_____

_____

_____

13.) When people get together in groups, it's easy for negative attitudes to slip in. How can you address these negative attitudes without hurting the ones you are addressing?

_____

_____

_____

_____

_____

_____

_____

14.) Sometimes toxins such as negativity, doubt, or fear can slip into life and relationships. What toxins are you facing in your life? What is your plan to address them?

_____

_____

_____

_____

_____

_____

_____

_____

_____

15.) In the parent-toddler analogy, the parent has three choices during a meltdown: "They can ignore the child, give in to their desires, or address the issue for the purpose of growth." As a leader and as a person, you have those same three choices on a daily basis. What do you naturally tend to do? What do you find most effective? Can you give some examples?

_____

_____

_____

_____

_____

_____

_____

_____

16.) Think about a time where you volunteered for something. What was the attitude of the atmosphere like?

_____

_____

_____

_____

_____

_____

_____

_____

17.) Share an example of a time when someone spoke words of life to you? How did it affect you?

_____

_____

_____

_____

_____

_____

_____

_____

Personal Reflection Questions:

18.) _____

_____

_____

_____

_____

_____

_____

_____

_____

_____

_____

_____

_____

19.) _____

Chapter 14
Nehemiah 12
Taking Care of People

Caring for people goes far beyond providing a paycheck or being kind when you see them once a week. Caring requires intentionality and genuinely getting to know the needs of people For leadership to be truly effective, people must feel valued and cared for. This can look very differently for different people. Make sure you are getting to know the person and not just what they can or can't do.

1.) Would you consider yourself to be a caring person? Would others agree or disagree with you and why?

_____

_____

_____

_____

_____

_____

_____

_____

_____

_____

_____

2.) What are some characteristics of a safe place or person you would go to in order to share life's ups and downs? Are you a safe person for others?

_____

_____

_____

_____

_____

_____

_____

_____

3.)   When listening to others share, do you focus on the problem mentioned or seek to help uncover the root of the problem? Share a story where the root was discovered or where you missed an opportunity to uncover the root because you focused only on the problem mentioned.

_____

_____

_____

_____

_____

_____

_____

_____

4.)   Explain the difference in sharing a problem to get to a solution versus gossip?

_____

_____

_____

_____

_____

_____

_____

_____

5.)   In order to build a caring culture, everyone must be on board with that happening. Each person must care for others in order to establish greater trust and respect. What are some ways that you can be a part of helping this type of culture to grow around you?

_____

_____

_____

_____

_____

_____

_____

_____

_____

6.)   What are ways that you or your company shows support during difficult times in the lives of those around you? What are new ways you can do so and what are times that you consider important for this to happen?

_____

_____

_____

_____

_____

_____

_____

_____

_____

7.) We live in a multi-culture society. In what ways do you need to learn to be culturally sensitive? Some examples may include dealing with conflict, celebrations, apologies, compliments, or social interaction.

_____

_____

_____

_____

_____

_____

_____

_____

8.) When people are going through major life changes, it may cause them to act or respond differently than they normally would. How do you remain balanced in this so that things get done, but grace is shown?

_____

_____

_____

_____

_____

_____

_____

_____

_____

_____

9.) There are several tests used to help determine one's personality or love language. If you have taken one of these, please share the results. How would sharing this with others and knowing the results of the people around you be beneficial?

_____

_____

_____

_____

_____

_____

_____

10.) It does not take much for money to cause rifts in relationships. Money can be used to bless and it can be used as a curse. Share some examples of how money has built or destroyed people.

_____

_____

_____

_____

_____

_____

_____

11.) What does it mean to be transparent with your finances? Are your finances transparent with those that need to be able to trust you in that area?

_____

_____

_____

_____

_____

_____

_____

_____

_____

12.) Helping those within your influence flourish and live well does not always mean giving money to people. Are you investing in people's lives and helping them get the knowledge and resources they need to improve and develop? What are some helpful resources you've found along the way?

_____

_____

_____

_____

_____

_____

_____

_____

_____

_____

13.) How are you doing in noticing the people around you by doing things such as saying hello or calling them by name? Share some additional examples of how you do this.

_____

_____

_____

_____

_____

_____

_____

_____

_____

14.) Once this culture of care has been established, what are things you can do to make sure people don't become lax in it and slip back into solitary living?

_____

_____

_____

_____

_____

_____

_____

_____

_____

15.) Are there people that you need to forgive so that the relationship can move forward and you can care for them well?

_____

_____

_____

_____

_____

_____

_____

_____

_____

16.) Do you feel cared for and valued? Explain why or how you feel this way.

_____

_____

_____

_____

_____

_____

_____

_____

_____

Personal Reflection Questions:

17.) _____

_____

_____

_____

_____

_____

_____

_____

_____

_____

_____

_____

_____

_____

18.) _____

_____

_____

_____

_____

_____

_____

_____

_____

_____

_____

_____

_____

Chapter 15
Nehemiah 13
Conflict Management

Quite often when people hear the word "conflict" they instantly have a negative understanding of the word. Conflict, however, does not have to be bad. Conflict has caused some of the greatest changes and ideas in our world, and often strengthens relationships when solutions are found that are mutually beneficial. As you look at conflict, I challenge you to see it as a chance for growth instead of as a barrier.

1.) What has been your historical approach to conflict? Do you embrace it, run from it, explode when it happens, etc...? What would others say you do?

_____

_____

_____

_____

_____

_____

_____

2.) What are some ways your family dealt with conflict when you were growing up? Share an example.

_____

_____

_____

_____

_____

_____

_____

_____

_____

3.) What would be the result of healthy conflict management?

_____

_____

_____

_____

_____

_____

4.) From Nehemiah chapter 13, briefly describe the conflict Nehemiah faced and how he responded.

_____

_____

_____

_____

_____

_____

_____

5.) It is easy to look at the problem and not see the person behind it. What are some ways you can make sure to keep the person in mind as you deal with the conflict?

_____

_____

_____

_____

_____

_____

6.) How can you see set standards being beneficial in dealing with conflict as it arises?

_____

_____

_____

_____

_____

_____

_____

_____

_____

_____

_____

_____

7.) Isolating the source of the conflict is very important, especially in groups. Share a time when you saw this done well or poorly. If poorly, what are ways it could have been handled better?

_____

_____

_____

_____

_____

_____

_____

_____

8.) Keeping conflict quiet helps people build their trust in you and provides opportunities for them to really learn and grow from mistakes or problems. What are some ways you can work to improve this in your life? Share an example of a person who was publically addressed in a negative way and how it affected them personally.

_____

_____

_____

_____

_____

_____

_____

_____

_____

_____

9.) Dealing with conflict lovingly does not mean that there are no consequences to behaviors. Do you have a standard for consequences in your workplace, home, or group that everyone is clear on? Without standards, it's easy to give unjust consequences based out of emotions or public opinions.

_____

_____

_____

_____

_____

_____

_____

_____

10.) When problems arise, how quick are you in responding to them? Do people feel that you will help bring resolution? Why do they hold this opinion?

_____

_____

_____

_____

_____

_____

_____

_____

_____

11.) If at the end of conflict resolution, the problem is solved and the relationship is intact, you have achieved the best result. This, however requires both sides to be willing to cooperate and have the same desire of keeping the relationship. How do you respond when this is not the case?

_____

_____

_____

_____

_____

_____

_____

_____

_____

_____

_____

_____

12.) In approaching conflict, one of the best things you can do is ask questions to really understand what is going on. What are some good questions you can ask or have been asked of you?

_____

_____

_____

_____

_____

_____

_____

_____

_____

Personal Reflection Questions:

13.) _____

_____

_____

_____

_____

_____

_____

_____

_____

_____

_____

_____

_____

_____

14.) _____

_____

_____

_____

_____

_____

_____

_____

_____

_____

_____

_____

_____

_____

Chapter 16
Nehemiah 13:15-30
Building and Maintaining Quality Relationships

Once you've established relationships, the growth of those are dependent upon you and how much you're willing to invest to see it develop. The quality of the relationship requires both people being willing to be open and to give of time. It takes work, but you don't have to feel the pressure of developing deep, meaningful relationships with everyone. Be wise in knowing how much time you have to give and who you need to invest more time in. Determine which relationships need to be at which level and draw in close those who will encourage you and those you've committed to. When you are over or under extended, you cannot be a full benefit to anyone.

1.)   How can doing the right thing at the wrong time be harmful to someone? Share a time when this happened.

_____

_____

_____

_____

_____

_____

_____

_____

2.)   Who are you currently spending a lot of time with?

_____

_____

_____

_____

_____

_____

_____

3.) Who do you need to be investing time in?

_____

_____

_____

_____

_____

_____

_____

_____

4.) Do these two lists align? What changes need to be made and what is your plan for doing that?

_____

_____

_____

_____

_____

_____

_____

_____

_____

5.) Are you willing to confront actions that are out of standard or do not meet your expectations? How do you usually approach those conversations?

_____

_____

_____

_____

_____

6.) When faced with difficult decisions, are you willing to stand for what is right or do you give in to the pressure and make poor decisions just to please people? Share an example.

_____

_____

_____

_____

_____

_____

_____

_____

7.) Do you use conflict and complaints from others as opportunities to grow? If so, what does this look like in your life? If not, what are ways you can grow in this area?

_____

_____

_____

_____

_____

_____

8.) What are some "wastes" in your life that you could minimize?

_____

_____

_____

_____

9.) Are you open to having those close to you point out wastes in your life and vice versa? If yes, how have you seen this effective in growing you? If not, what keeps you from it?

_____

_____

_____

_____

_____

_____

_____

10.) If you fail to meet standards in your own life and relationships, what are things you can do to help restore broken trust and reestablish commitment?

_____

_____

_____

_____

_____

_____

_____

11.) "Choose to see the heart of the person and not just their actions. Be quick to forgive and slow to anger." This can be very difficult to do. Can you share a time when you've seen this lived out well and what were the benefits?

_____

_____

_____

_____

_____

_____

_____

_____

12.) 1 Corinthians 15:33 says, "Do not be deceived: "Bad company ruins good morals."' (ESV)" As you think about those you allow in your inner circle, what type of characteristics are they instilling in you? What type of characteristics are you instilling in them?

_____

_____

_____

_____

_____

_____

_____

_____

_____

13.) List some characteristics of the value system that you desire to have and display to others.

_____

_____

_____

_____

_____

_____

_____

_____

_____

14.) When people talk about how you have influenced them and impacted their lives, what do they say? If this is not the legacy you want to leave behind, what are some things you can change?

_____

_____

_____

_____

_____

_____

_____

_____

15.) Who are some people who have greatly influenced your values for the good and helped build character in you? What was it about their lives, words or actions that helped mold you?

_____

_____

_____

_____

_____

_____

_____

_____

_____

_____

_____

_____

_____

16.) Are you encouraging the growth of those around you? Are you inspiring them to develop as a person in character and values?

_____

_____

_____

_____

_____

_____

_____

_____

_____

17.) Are you currently the person you want to be? Are you becoming the person you want to be? What are your goals in these areas and your plan to attain them?

_____

_____

_____

_____

_____

_____

_____

_____

_____

_____

Personal Reflection Questions:

18.) _____

_____

_____

_____

_____

_____

_____

_____

_____

_____

_____

_____

_____

_____

19.) _____

_____

_____

_____

_____

_____

_____

_____

_____

_____

_____

_____

_____

_____

_____

_____

_____

_____

_____

Chapter 17
Conclusion

You can make a difference. You can develop, inspire, encourage, and grow other people. You can be a part of transforming lives. Some of you will easily believe that and carry on as you have been doing with a little boost in your step. Others of you will doubt that you can really be used to help others. I'd like to ask you to write a letter to yourself. Speak to your heart and tell yourself what it is about you that can be used for the good of others. Write out your goals for personal growth where you clarify your hoshins and develop your steps to help you reach those goals. Share these with someone that can help you PDCA your plan along the way in order to keep you moving forward. Set times to discuss them and make sure standards and expectations are clear. If you want to build a wall, you have to start laying bricks.

Dear Self,

_____

_____

_____

_____

_____

_____

_____

_____

_____

_____

_____

_____

_____

_____

_____

_____

_____

_____

_____

_____

_____

_____

_____

_____

_____

_____

_____

_____

_____

_____

_____

_____

_____

_____

_____

_____

_____

_____

References

Ford, Henry. *Henry Ford Quotes.* n.d.
https://www.google.com/url?sa=t&rct=j&q=&esrc=s&source=web&cd=6&cad
=rja&uact=8&ved=0CD0QFjAF&url=https%3A%2F%2Fmedia.ford.com%2Fcont
ent%2Ffordmedia%2Ffna%2Fus%2Fen%2Fasset.download.document.pdf.html%
2Fcontent%2Fdam%2Ffordmedia%2FNorth%2520America%2FUS%2F2.

Kipling, Rudyard. *Rewards and Fairies.* First. Garden City: Doubleday, 1910.

Sloan, Dave. *Millennials are changing jobs at a less frequent rate than prior generations.*
September 4, 2014. http://www.pbs.org/newshour/rundown/millennials-
changing-jobs-less-frequent-rate-prior-generations/.

www.ingramcontent.com/pod-product-compliance
Lightning Source LLC
Chambersburg PA
CBHW051413200326

41520CB00023B/7216